INTRODUCTION TO LITHOPS PLA................

ORIGIN AND NATURAL HABITAT OF LITHOPS 5

UNDERSTANDING THE MORPHOLOGY AND ANATOMY OF LITHOPS...7

DIFFERENT TYPES OF LITHOPS 9

CHOOSING THE RIGHT SOIL MIX FOR LITHOPS.................11

UNDERSTANDING THE WATERING NEEDS OF LITHOPS....13

IDEAL LIGHT CONDITIONS FOR LITHOPS 15

THE ROLE OF TEMPERATURE AND HUMIDITY IN LITHOPS GROWTH..17

PROPAGATION TECHNIQUES FOR LITHOPS 19

IDEAL TIME FOR PROPAGATING LITHOPS 22

GROWING LITHOPS FROM SEED 24

GRAFTING LITHOPS 26

TOOLS REQUIRED FOR LITHOPS PROPAGATION 28

THE IMPORTANCE OF PROPER TRANSPLANTING OF LITHOPS..30

COMMON PESTS AND DISEASES OF LITHOPS 32

SYMPTOMS AND SIGNS OF LITHOPS DISEASES 35

PREVENTION AND TREATMENT OF LITHOPS DISEASES ...37

FERTILIZING LITHOPS 39

DIFFERENT TYPES OF FERTILIZERS FOR LITHOPS 41

UNDERSTANDING THE NUTRITIONAL NEEDS OF LITHOPS 44

PRUNING LITHOPS...46

BENEFITS OF PRUNING LITHOPS 48

HARVESTING LITHOPS 49

USES OF LITHOPS 51

CREATING AN ATTRACTIVE LITHOPS DISPLAY 52

IDEAL CONTAINERS FOR LITHOPS 54

LANDSCAPING WITH LITHOPS 56

TIPS FOR SUCCESSFUL LITHOPS CULTIVATION 59

CONCLUSION 61

INTRODUCTION TO LITHOPS PLANT

Lithops is a genus of succulent plants native to southern Africa. They are also known as living stones or stone plants because of their remarkable resemblance to rocks. Lithops plants are popular among succulent enthusiasts due to their unique appearance and relatively low maintenance requirements.

APPEARANCE

Lithops plants typically have a flattened, almost disc-like shape and grow very close to the ground. They are usually small, ranging in size from about 1 to 10 centimeters in diameter. Lithops have a thick, fleshy, and water-retentive surface that helps them survive in their arid environment. Their leaves are often patterned and come in a range of colors, including shades of green, brown, gray, and red.

CULTIVATION

Lithops plants are relatively easy to grow and care for, making them a popular choice for indoor and outdoor gardens. They prefer well-draining soil, bright but filtered light, and moderate watering. Lithops are adapted to survive in a dry climate, so overwatering should be avoided to prevent root rot. They also require little fertilizer and should only be fed sparingly during the growing season.

PROPAGATION

Lithops can be propagated by division or seed. Division involves separating a mature plant into smaller parts and replanting them in separate containers. Seeds can be sown in well-draining soil and kept moist until they germinate. It is important to note that Lithops seeds can take several weeks to germinate and require patience.

ORIGIN AND NATURAL HABITAT OF LITHOPS

Lithops is a genus of succulent plants that are native to southern Africa. They are found in a variety of habitats, including deserts, rocky outcrops, and savannas. Lithops plants are adapted to survive in arid and semi-arid environments, where water is scarce and temperatures can be extreme.

GEOGRAPHIC DISTRIBUTION

The natural range of Lithops plants extends from southern Namibia, through South Africa, and into the northern parts of Botswana and Swaziland. They are most commonly found in the western and southern regions of South Africa, where they grow in a variety of soil types, including sand, gravel, and shale.

HABITAT

Lithops plants are well adapted to survive in their harsh environment. They have a thick, fleshy surface that helps them retain water and allows them to survive periods of drought. They also have a unique camouflage that helps them blend in with their surroundings, making them difficult to spot by predators. Lithops are often found growing in groups or colonies, which provide protection and help to regulate temperature and humidity levels.

ECOLOGICAL IMPORTANCE

Lithops plants play an important role in their ecosystem. They are a source of food and shelter for a variety of insects and animals, including beetles, ants, and small rodents. They also help to prevent soil erosion by stabilizing the soil with their roots. In addition, Lithops plants are often used in traditional medicine to treat a variety of ailments, including coughs, colds, and skin infections.

UNDERSTANDING THE MORPHOLOGY AND ANATOMY OF LITHOPS

Lithops is a genus of succulent plants that have a unique morphology and anatomy. Understanding the structure of Lithops plants can help in their cultivation and care.

MORPHOLOGY

Lithops plants have a flattened, almost disc-like shape and grow very close to the ground. The top of the plant is covered with two thick, fleshy leaves that are fused together to form a single body known as a pair of leaves. The pair of leaves is often patterned and comes in a range of colors, including shades of green, brown, gray, and red. Lithops also have a small fissure, or slit, between the pair of leaves that allows light to enter and helps with photosynthesis.

ANATOMY

Lithops plants have a unique anatomy that allows them to survive in arid and semi-arid environments. They have a thick, water-retentive surface that helps them retain moisture and survive periods of drought. The inside of the plant is made up of a compact network of cells that are filled with water-storing tissue. Lithops plants also have a shallow root system that spreads out horizontally to absorb as much water as possible from the soil.

REPRODUCTION

Lithops plants reproduce through a process known as sexual reproduction. They produce flowers that are small and usually white or yellow in color. The flowers are pollinated by insects and produce a fruit that contains several seeds. Lithops seeds are very small and can take several weeks to germinate. Once the seeds have germinated, they will begin to grow into new plants.

DIFFERENT TYPES OF LITHOPS

Lithops is a genus of succulent plants that includes many different species and cultivars. Each type of Lithops has its own unique characteristics and appearance.

LITHOPS KARASMONTANA

Lithops karasmontana is a species of Lithops that is native to Namibia. It is a small plant that usually grows to around 3 centimeters in diameter. The pair of leaves is usually grayish-green in color and has a rough, pebbled texture. Lithops karasmontana is a popular species among collectors because of its unique appearance.

LITHOPS AUCAMPIAE

Lithops aucampiae is a species of Lithops that is native to South Africa. It is a medium-sized plant that usually grows to around 5 centimeters in diameter. The pair of leaves is usually reddish-brown in color and has a smooth, shiny texture. Lithops aucampiae is a popular species among collectors because of its striking coloration.

LITHOPS SALICOLA

Lithops salicola is a species of Lithops that is native to South Africa. It is a small plant that usually grows to around 2 centimeters in diameter. The pair of leaves is usually greenish-brown in color and has a smooth, shiny texture. Lithops salicola is a popular species among collectors because of its compact size and interesting shape.

CULTIVARS

In addition to the different species of Lithops, there are also many different cultivars available. Cultivars are plants that have been bred for specific traits, such as color or pattern. Some popular Lithops cultivars include Lithops 'Livingstonei', which has a striking red and green coloration, and Lithops 'Pseudotruncatella', which has a unique flattened shape.

CHOOSING THE RIGHT SOIL MIX FOR LITHOPS

Lithops are succulent plants that require well-draining soil to thrive. Choosing the right soil mix for your Lithops plants is essential for their health and growth.

INGREDIENTS

A good soil mix for Lithops should be made up of a combination of materials that promote drainage and prevent waterlogging. Some common ingredients for Lithops soil mixes include:

- Coarse sand or grit
- Perlite
- Pumice
- Volcanic rock
- Gravel

PROPORTIONS

The proportions of each ingredient in your Lithops soil mix will depend on your climate and growing conditions. In general, a good rule of thumb is to use a mix that is around 70-80% inorganic material and 20-30% organic material. This will provide enough nutrients for your plants without holding onto too much moisture.

PREPARATION

To prepare your Lithops soil mix, simply combine the ingredients in a large container and mix well. You can also add a small amount of slow-release fertilizer to provide additional nutrients for your plants. It's important to use gloves and a mask when mixing your soil to avoid inhaling any dust or particles.

TESTING YOUR MIX

Before potting your Lithops plants, it's a good idea to test your soil mix for drainage. To do this, wet your soil mix and let it drain completely. Then, press your finger into the soil to create a small hole. If the hole stays intact and doesn't collapse, your soil mix is well-draining and suitable for Lithops. If the hole collapses, you may need to add more inorganic material to improve drainage.

UNDERSTANDING THE WATERING NEEDS OF LITHOPS

Watering Lithops can be tricky, as these succulent plants are adapted to survive in arid conditions with very little rainfall. Overwatering can lead to root rot and other issues, so it's important to understand the watering needs of Lithops.

FREQUENCY

Lithops should be watered infrequently, usually no more than once every two to three weeks during the growing season (spring and summer) and once every one to two months during the dormant season (fall and winter). However, the frequency of watering will depend on your climate and growing conditions.

AMOUNT

When watering Lithops, it's important to give them enough water to thoroughly wet the soil, but not so much that the soil becomes waterlogged. A good rule of thumb is to water until the soil is moist but not soggy. You can also use a moisture meter or stick to check the moisture level of the soil before watering.

METHOD

One effective method of watering Lithops is the "soak and dry" method. To do this, water your plants until the soil is thoroughly wet, then allow the soil to dry out completely before watering again. This method mimics the natural rainfall patterns in the plants' native habitat and helps prevent overwatering.

TIPS

Here are some additional tips to keep in mind when watering Lithops:

- Water in the morning or early afternoon to allow any excess moisture to evaporate before nightfall.
- Avoid getting water on the leaves, as this can lead to rot and other issues.
- Use a well-draining soil mix to prevent waterlogging.
- Reduce watering during the dormant season to avoid excessive moisture in the soil.

IDEAL LIGHT CONDITIONS FOR LITHOPS

Lithops require bright, direct sunlight to thrive. However, it's important to be mindful of the intensity of light and the duration of exposure to avoid damaging the plants.

INTENSITY

The intensity of light that Lithops require varies depending on their species and natural habitat. In general, they prefer bright, direct sunlight for several hours a day. However, too much direct sunlight can cause sunburn and scorching, so it's important to gradually acclimate your plants to full sun exposure over time.

DURATION

The duration of exposure to sunlight also depends on the species of Lithops and the time of year. During the summer months, when the days are longer and the sun is more intense, Lithops can handle longer periods of direct sunlight. However, during the winter months, when the days are shorter and the sun is weaker, they may require less direct sunlight to prevent sunburn and other issues.

INDOOR VS. OUTDOOR LIGHT

If you're growing Lithops indoors, it's important to provide them with bright, direct sunlight for several hours a day. This can be achieved by placing them near a south-facing window or using grow lights to simulate natural sunlight. Outdoor Lithops should be placed in a sunny, well-ventilated location, such as a south-facing balcony or patio.

TIPS

Here are some additional tips to keep in mind when providing light for your Lithops:

- Avoid exposing Lithops to intense sunlight during the hottest part of the day, as this can cause damage.
- Gradually acclimate your plants to full sun exposure over time.
- Provide shade or protection during extreme heat waves or intense sun exposure.
- Rotate your plants regularly to ensure that all sides receive adequate sunlight.

THE ROLE OF TEMPERATURE AND HUMIDITY IN LITHOPS GROWTH

Temperature and humidity are important factors to consider when growing Lithops. These plants are adapted to survive in arid conditions with hot days and cool nights, so it's important to provide them with similar conditions to promote healthy growth.

TEMPERATURE

Lithops prefer warm temperatures during the day and cooler temperatures at night. In their natural habitat, daytime temperatures can reach up to 90°F (32°C), while nighttime temperatures can drop to as low as 40°F (4°C). To mimic these conditions, it's important to provide Lithops with a warm, sunny location during the day and a cooler location at night.

During the winter months, it's important to provide Lithops with cooler temperatures to promote dormancy. This can be achieved by placing them in a cooler room or by reducing the temperature of their growing environment.

HUMIDITY

Lithops are adapted to survive in arid conditions with low humidity. In fact, too much humidity can lead to fungal and bacterial issues, so it's important to provide Lithops with a dry, well-ventilated environment.

During the growing season, it's important to avoid overwatering and to allow the soil to dry out completely between waterings. This helps prevent excessive humidity in the soil and promotes healthy root growth.

TIPS

Here are some additional tips to keep in mind when considering the role of temperature and humidity in Lithops growth:

- Provide Lithops with a warm, sunny location during the day and a cooler location at night to mimic their natural habitat.
- During the winter months, provide Lithops with cooler temperatures to promote dormancy.
- Avoid overwatering and allow the soil to dry out completely between waterings to prevent excessive humidity.
- Provide a dry, well-ventilated environment to promote healthy growth and prevent fungal and bacterial issues.

PROPAGATION TECHNIQUES FOR LITHOPS

Lithops can be propagated through various techniques, including seed propagation and division of mature plants.

SEED PROPAGATION

Seed propagation is the most common method of propagating Lithops. To propagate Lithops from seed, follow these steps:

1. Obtain fresh Lithops seeds from a reputable source.
2. Prepare a well-draining soil mixture using a combination of sand, perlite, and a small amount of peat moss.
3. Sow the seeds on the surface of the soil mixture and press them lightly into the soil.
4. Water the soil lightly and cover the container with plastic wrap to create a humid environment.
5. Place the container in a warm, bright location and keep the soil moist but not waterlogged.
6. The seeds should germinate in 1-3 weeks, depending on the species and growing conditions.
7. Once the seedlings have developed their first set of true leaves, they can be transplanted into individual containers.

DIVISION OF MATURE PLANTS

Division of mature Lithops plants is another method of propagation. To propagate Lithops through division, follow these steps:

1. Carefully remove the entire plant from its container and gently shake off any excess soil.
2. Inspect the plant for any signs of damage or disease.
3. Using a sharp, clean knife, carefully divide the plant into two or more sections, making sure that each section has at least one healthy root system and a few healthy leaves.
4. Allow the cut surfaces to dry for a few days.
5. Prepare a well-draining soil mixture using a combination of sand, perlite, and a small amount of peat moss.
6. Plant each section in its own container and water lightly.
7. Place the containers in a warm, bright location and keep the soil moist but not waterlogged.
8. The new plants should establish themselves within a few weeks to a few months, depending on the species and growing conditions.

TIPS

Here are some additional tips to keep in mind when propagating Lithops:

- Use fresh seeds from a reputable source to ensure viability.
- Be careful not to overwater the soil, as this can cause the seeds or cuttings to rot.
- Allow the cut surfaces of divided plants to dry completely before planting to prevent rot.
- Transplant seedlings or new divisions into individual containers once they have developed their first set of true leaves.
- Be patient, as it may take several weeks to several months for new plants to establish themselves.

IDEAL TIME FOR PROPAGATING LITHOPS

The ideal time to propagate Lithops depends on the specific propagation method and the climate in which you live.

SEED PROPAGATION

Seed propagation can be done year-round, but the best time to sow Lithops seeds is during the spring or fall. This is when temperatures are moderate and the days are shorter, which can help encourage germination.

DIVISION OF MATURE PLANTS

Division of mature Lithops plants is best done during the summer months when the plants are actively growing. Avoid dividing the plants during the winter months when they are dormant, as this can stress the plant and reduce its chances of survival.

TIPS

Here are some additional tips to keep in mind when propagating Lithops:

- Choose the propagation method that works best for you and your climate.
- Make sure to provide the right growing conditions for your Lithops, such as adequate light, water, and temperature.

- Be patient and give your Lithops time to establish itself, especially when propagating through seeds.

GROWING LITHOPS FROM SEED

MATERIALS NEEDED

- Lithops seeds
- Well-draining soil mix (such as a 50/50 mix of perlite and potting soil)
- Pot or container with drainage holes
- Plastic wrap or lid
- Mister or spray bottle

STEPS

1. Fill the pot or container with the well-draining soil mix and moisten the soil slightly with a mister or spray bottle.
2. Scatter the Lithops seeds on top of the soil mix and cover them lightly with a thin layer of soil mix.
3. Cover the pot or container with plastic wrap or a lid to create a humid environment.
4. Place the pot or container in a bright location with indirect sunlight and temperatures between 60-75°F (15-24°C).
5. Mist the soil with water whenever it starts to dry out, but be careful not to overwater and keep the soil slightly moist.
6. After 2-4 weeks, the Lithops seeds should start to germinate. Once the seedlings have developed their second pair of leaves, remove the plastic wrap or lid.
7. Continue to care for the Lithops seedlings as they grow, gradually reducing the frequency of watering and increasing their exposure to sunlight.
8. Once the Lithops seedlings have developed their true leaves and have grown to a size of about 1 inch (2.5 cm) in diameter, they can be transplanted into individual pots or containers.

TIPS

- Make sure to use well-draining soil mix and avoid overwatering to prevent root rot.
- Be patient, as Lithops seeds can take several weeks or even months to germinate.
- Provide enough light, but avoid direct sunlight, which can cause the seedlings to burn.
- As the Lithops seedlings grow, make sure to keep them separated to avoid overcrowding and competition for nutrients.

GRAFTING LITHOPS

MATERIALS NEEDED

- A mature Lithops plant as the scion (the top part of the graft)
- A rootstock plant (such as Hylocereus cactus or Pereskiopsis) to use as the base of the graft
- A sharp, sterile knife or blade
- Grafting tape or rubber bands
- Optional: rooting hormone

STEPS

1. Choose a healthy, mature Lithops plant to use as the scion.
2. Choose a suitable rootstock plant and make a clean, straight cut at the desired location for the graft.
3. Make a matching, clean cut on the Lithops scion.
4. Optional: apply rooting hormone to the cut surface of the Lithops scion.
5. Place the Lithops scion onto the cut surface of the rootstock plant, making sure that the cuts match up as closely as possible.
6. Secure the graft in place using grafting tape or rubber bands, making sure not to overtighten or damage the plant.
7. Keep the graft in a warm, dry location with indirect sunlight for several days to allow it to heal and begin growing.
8. Once the graft has begun to grow, gradually increase its exposure to light and water, taking care not to overwater or let the soil dry out completely.

TIPS

- Choose a rootstock plant that is healthy and compatible with Lithops, such as Hylocereus cactus or Pereskiopsis.

- Use a sharp, sterile knife or blade to make clean cuts to prevent infection and damage to the plant.
- Consider using rooting hormone to encourage faster and stronger growth.
- Monitor the graft carefully for signs of stress or infection, such as wilting or discoloration, and take appropriate action if necessary.

TOOLS REQUIRED FOR LITHOPS PROPAGATION

MATERIALS NEEDED

- Sharp, sterile knife or blade
- Cutting board or surface
- Pot or container for planting
- Succulent or cactus soil mix
- Optional: rooting hormone

STEPS

1. Choose a healthy Lithops plant to propagate.
2. Prepare a clean, flat surface to work on and gather your materials.
3. Using a sharp, sterile knife or blade, carefully cut the Lithops plant at the desired location for propagation.
4. Allow the cut to callus over for a few days to reduce the risk of infection.
5. Plant the cut Lithops in a pot or container filled with a well-draining succulent or cactus soil mix.
6. Water the soil lightly, being careful not to overwater or let the soil become waterlogged.
7. Optional: apply rooting hormone to the cut end of the Lithops before planting to encourage faster and stronger growth.
8. Place the newly propagated Lithops in a bright, warm location with indirect sunlight.

TIPS

- Always use a sharp, sterile knife or blade to prevent infection and damage to the plant.
- Allow the cut to callus over for a few days before planting to reduce the risk of infection.
- Choose a well-draining soil mix to prevent waterlogged soil and root rot.
- Water the newly propagated Lithops lightly and gradually increase watering as the plant grows.
- Monitor the plant closely for signs of stress or infection, such as wilting or discoloration, and take appropriate action if necessary.

THE IMPORTANCE OF PROPER TRANSPLANTING OF LITHOPS

WHY IS PROPER TRANSPLANTING IMPORTANT?

Proper transplanting is crucial for the health and survival of Lithops plants. These plants have unique root systems and are sensitive to disturbance, making them more vulnerable to stress and injury during transplanting. Without proper care and attention, Lithops can suffer from transplant shock and may not recover.

WHEN TO TRANSPLANT LITHOPS?

Lithops should only be transplanted when absolutely necessary, such as when the plant outgrows its current container or when the soil has become depleted and is no longer providing the necessary nutrients. It's best to transplant Lithops during their active growth period in the spring or fall to give the plant time to recover and adjust before the harsher summer or winter months.

STEPS FOR PROPER TRANSPLANTING

1. Choose a new container that is slightly larger than the current one to allow for growth.
2. Prepare a well-draining soil mix that is suitable for Lithops.

3. Carefully remove the Lithops plant from its current container, being sure to avoid damaging the roots or stem.
4. Gently loosen any tangled or compacted roots, and remove any dead or damaged roots.
5. Place the Lithops in the center of the new container, and fill in the gaps with the prepared soil mix.
6. Lightly tamp down the soil and water the plant.
7. Place the newly transplanted Lithops in a bright, warm location with indirect sunlight and avoid watering for a few days to allow the plant to adjust.

TIPS FOR SUCCESSFUL TRANSPLANTING

- Use a well-draining soil mix to prevent waterlogged soil and root rot.
- Transplant Lithops during their active growth period in the spring or fall to give the plant time to adjust.
- Handle the plant gently and avoid damaging the roots or stem.
- Water the plant lightly after transplanting, and avoid overwatering.
- Monitor the plant closely for signs of stress or infection, such as wilting or discoloration, and take appropriate action if necessary.

COMMON PESTS AND DISEASES OF LITHOPS

PESTS

MEALYBUGS

Mealybugs are small, white, cotton-like insects that often appear in clusters on the leaves or stems of Lithops. They feed on the sap of the plant and can cause stunted growth, yellowing, and wilting. To control mealybugs, remove them manually with a cotton swab or neem oil.

SPIDER MITES

Spider mites are tiny arachnids that are difficult to spot with the naked eye. They often appear as a fine webbing on the leaves of Lithops and can cause yellowing and wilting. To control spider mites, rinse the plant with a strong stream of water or use neem oil.

SCALE INSECTS

Scale insects are small, oval-shaped insects that attach themselves to the leaves and stems of Lithops. They feed on the sap of the plant and can cause yellowing and wilting. To control scale insects, remove them manually with a cotton swab or neem oil.

DISEASES

ROOT ROT

Root rot is a fungal disease that can affect Lithops if the soil is too moist and poorly drained. It causes the roots to rot and can lead to wilting and death of the plant. To prevent root rot, use a well-draining soil mix and avoid overwatering the plant.

LEAF SPOT

Leaf spot is a fungal disease that can affect Lithops if the plant is exposed to too much moisture. It causes brown or black spots on the leaves and can lead to wilting and death of the plant. To prevent leaf spot, avoid getting water on the leaves and ensure proper air circulation around the plant.

VIRUS

Virus can also affect Lithops, causing distorted growth and discoloration of the leaves. There is no cure for viral infections, so infected plants should be removed to prevent the spread of the virus to healthy plants.

PREVENTION

The best way to prevent pests and diseases from affecting Lithops is to maintain good growing conditions, including providing proper light, watering, and soil conditions. Regularly inspecting the plant for signs of pests and diseases can also help catch and treat problems early on.

SYMPTOMS AND SIGNS OF LITHOPS DISEASES

ROOT ROT

SYMPTOMS

- Yellowing of leaves
- Soft, mushy, or blackened roots
- Stunted growth
- Wilting

SIGNS

- Foul odor from the soil
- Mold or fungus on the soil surface

LEAF SPOT

SYMPTOMS

- Brown or black spots on leaves
- Yellowing of leaves
- Wilting

SIGNS

- Fungus or mold growth on affected leaves

VIRUS

SYMPTOMS

- Distorted or misshapen leaves
- Discoloration of leaves
- Stunted growth

SIGNS

- No visible signs, as viruses are too small to be seen with the naked eye

PREVENTION AND TREATMENT

The best way to prevent diseases in Lithops is to provide proper growing conditions, including well-draining soil, proper watering, and adequate light. If you suspect your Lithops is diseased, remove the affected leaves or plant and treat the soil with a fungicide or bactericide. If the disease has spread extensively, it may be necessary to remove the entire plant to prevent the spread to other plants.

PREVENTION AND TREATMENT OF LITHOPS DISEASES

PREVENTION

Preventing Lithops diseases involves providing the proper growing conditions. Ensure that you use a well-draining soil mix, water the plant only when the soil is completely dry, provide adequate light, and avoid overcrowding the plants.

TREATMENT

If your Lithops plant shows signs of disease, act quickly to prevent the disease from spreading to other plants. Treatment options depend on the specific disease.

ROOT ROT

If root rot is suspected, remove the affected plant from the soil and discard the affected roots. Allow the plant to dry for several days before repotting it in a new, well-draining soil mix. Avoid overwatering the plant in the future.

LEAF SPOT

To treat leaf spot, remove the affected leaves and discard them. Treat the plant with a fungicide to prevent further spread of the disease.

VIRUS

There is no cure for a viral infection in plants. Infected plants should be immediately removed and destroyed to prevent the spread of the virus to other plants.

It is important to always use sterile tools when working with Lithops plants to prevent the spread of disease. Additionally, avoid over-fertilizing the plants, as this can weaken them and make them more susceptible to disease.

FERTILIZING LITHOPS

INTRODUCTION

Lithops are low-maintenance plants that do not require a lot of fertilizer. In fact, over-fertilizing can harm the plant. However, a small amount of fertilizer can help promote healthy growth and flowering.

WHEN TO FERTILIZE

Lithops should only be fertilized during their active growing season, which is typically in the spring and fall. Avoid fertilizing during the summer or winter, when the plants are dormant.

WHAT TO USE

A balanced, low-nitrogen fertilizer is best for Lithops. A 10-10-10 or 5-10-5 fertilizer can be used, but it should be diluted to half strength before application. Organic fertilizers, such as fish emulsion or compost tea, can also be used.

HOW TO APPLY

Fertilizer should be applied sparingly and evenly to the soil surface around the base of the plant. Avoid getting fertilizer on the leaves, as it can cause burn marks. Water the plant lightly after fertilizing to help distribute the fertilizer throughout the soil.

ADDITIONAL TIPS

It is important to never fertilize a newly transplanted Lithops until it has had time to acclimate to its new soil and environment. Additionally, avoid fertilizing Lithops that are stressed or not growing well, as this can further harm the plant.

DIFFERENT TYPES OF FERTILIZERS FOR LITHOPS

INTRODUCTION

Lithops are succulent plants that require very little fertilizer. However, when fertilizer is needed, it is important to use the right type of fertilizer in order to avoid damaging the plant. There are several types of fertilizers that can be used for Lithops, each with its own benefits and drawbacks.

ORGANIC FERTILIZERS

Organic fertilizers are derived from natural sources, such as plant or animal matter. They are generally considered to be safer and more environmentally friendly than synthetic fertilizers. Examples of organic fertilizers that can be used for Lithops include compost, compost tea, fish emulsion, and worm castings. Organic fertilizers are slow-acting and release nutrients over time, which can be beneficial for Lithops.

SYNTHETIC FERTILIZERS

Synthetic fertilizers are manufactured using chemical processes. They are typically less expensive than organic fertilizers and can provide quick results. However, they can also be harmful to the environment and can burn the roots of Lithops if used improperly. Examples of synthetic fertilizers that can be used for Lithops include 10-10-10, 5-10-5, and 15-30-15. Synthetic fertilizers should be used sparingly and diluted to half strength before application.

SLOW-RELEASE FERTILIZERS

Slow-release fertilizers are designed to release nutrients over an extended period of time, reducing the need for frequent fertilization. These fertilizers are available in both organic and synthetic forms. Slow-release fertilizers can be beneficial for Lithops, as they provide a consistent source of nutrients without the risk of over-fertilization. However, they can be more expensive than other types of fertilizers.

CACTUS AND SUCCULENT FERTILIZERS

Cactus and succulent fertilizers are specially formulated for plants like Lithops that require low levels of nitrogen and high levels of phosphorus and potassium. These fertilizers can be found at most garden centers and nurseries. Cactus and succulent fertilizers are typically less concentrated than other types of fertilizers, which can reduce the risk of over-fertilization. However, they can be more expensive than other types of fertilizers.

CONCLUSION

Choosing the right type of fertilizer for Lithops depends on the individual plant's needs and the gardener's preferences. Organic fertilizers are generally considered to be safer and more environmentally friendly, while synthetic fertilizers can provide quick results. Slow-release fertilizers can be beneficial for reducing the need for frequent fertilization, and cactus and succulent fertilizers are specially formulated for plants like Lithops. Regardless of the type of fertilizer used, it is important to apply it sparingly and to avoid over-fertilization, which can harm the plant.

UNDERSTANDING THE NUTRITIONAL NEEDS OF LITHOPS

NUTRIENTS REQUIRED BY LITHOPS

Like all plants, Lithops require a range of nutrients to grow and thrive. The primary macronutrients required by Lithops are nitrogen (N), phosphorus (P), and potassium (K), while secondary macronutrients include calcium (Ca), magnesium (Mg), and sulfur (S). Micronutrients are also essential for proper plant growth, although they are required in much smaller quantities than macronutrients. These include iron (Fe), manganese (Mn), zinc (Zn), copper (Cu), boron (B), and molybdenum (Mo).

HOW TO PROVIDE NUTRIENTS TO LITHOPS

Lithops can be fertilized using a variety of methods, including slow-release fertilizers, liquid fertilizers, and foliar sprays. Slow-release fertilizers are designed to release nutrients over an extended period, providing a steady supply of nutrients to the plant. Liquid fertilizers are dissolved in water and can be applied to the soil or sprayed directly onto the plant's leaves. Foliar sprays are designed to be sprayed directly onto the leaves, providing a quick source of nutrients that can be absorbed by the plant's leaves.

WHEN TO FERTILIZE LITHOPS

Lithops should be fertilized during their active growing season, which typically occurs in the spring and summer months. Fertilizing during this time can help promote healthy growth and flowering. It is important not to over-fertilize Lithops, as this can cause nutrient burn and other issues. It is generally recommended to fertilize Lithops once every 2-3 months during the growing season, using a balanced fertilizer that contains all essential nutrients. During the dormant season (fall and winter), Lithops do not require fertilization, as they are not actively growing.

PRUNING LITHOPS

WHY PRUNE LITHOPS?

Lithops generally do not require pruning, as they have a natural compact growth habit. However, there may be instances where pruning is necessary, such as: Removing dead or diseased plant material Removing offsets to promote plant growth and prevent overcrowding Shaping the plant for aesthetic purposes

HOW TO PRUNE LITHOPS

When pruning Lithops, it is important to use clean, sharp tools to prevent the spread of disease. Sterilize pruning tools by wiping them with rubbing alcohol or a solution of one part bleach to nine parts water. To remove dead or diseased plant material, use pruning shears or scissors to make a clean cut as close to the base of the plant as possible. Be sure to dispose of the pruned material properly to prevent the spread of disease. To remove offsets, use a sharp, sterile knife to carefully separate the offset from the parent plant. Allow the cut to dry for a few days before planting the offset in its own pot. If shaping the plant for aesthetic purposes, use pruning shears or scissors to make precise cuts as desired. Be sure to avoid cutting into the plant's meristem, as this can damage the plant and prevent future growth.

WHEN TO PRUNE LITHOPS

Pruning Lithops can be done at any time of the year, although it is generally best to wait until the plant's dormant season (fall and winter) to minimize stress on the plant. Avoid pruning during the plant's active growing season, as this can disrupt the plant's growth and flowering.

BENEFITS OF PRUNING LITHOPS

PROMOTES PLANT HEALTH

Pruning Lithops can help to promote plant health by removing dead or diseased plant material. This can prevent the spread of disease and also allow the plant to allocate its resources towards healthy growth.

PREVENTS OVERCROWDING

As Lithops produce offsets, the plant can become overcrowded over time. Pruning offsets can help to prevent overcrowding and ensure that the plant has enough space to grow and thrive.

ENHANCES AESTHETIC APPEARANCE

Pruning Lithops can also enhance the plant's aesthetic appearance by shaping it as desired. This can be especially useful for those who wish to create unique and visually appealing displays of their Lithops. Overall, pruning Lithops is a simple yet effective way to promote plant health, prevent overcrowding, and enhance the plant's aesthetic appearance.

HARVESTING LITHOPS

WHAT IS HARVESTING LITHOPS?

Harvesting Lithops refers to the process of collecting mature seeds from Lithops plants for propagation. This process is typically done in the fall after the Lithops have finished flowering.

HOW TO HARVEST LITHOPS?

To harvest Lithops seeds, wait until the seed capsules are fully mature and dry. The capsules will turn brown and split open, revealing the small, black seeds inside. Gently shake the capsules to release the seeds into a container.

STORING LITHOPS SEEDS

Once the seeds have been harvested, they should be stored in a cool, dry place until they are ready to be planted. It is important to store the seeds in an airtight container to prevent moisture from entering and causing the seeds to mold or rot.

WHEN TO PLANT LITHOPS SEEDS

Lithops seeds should be planted in the spring, as this is the time when the plants begin their active growth phase. Before planting, it is recommended to soak the seeds in water for a few hours to soften the outer seed coat and increase the chances of successful germination.

CONCLUSION

Harvesting Lithops seeds can be a rewarding and fun experience for those who enjoy propagating and growing these unique and fascinating plants. By following the proper techniques for harvesting and storing the seeds, Lithops enthusiasts can continue to grow and enjoy these plants for years to come.

USES OF LITHOPS

ORNAMENTAL USE

Lithops are primarily grown for their ornamental value. They are popular among succulent collectors and are often used in rock gardens, succulent gardens, and as indoor plants.

EDUCATION AND RESEARCH

Lithops are also used for educational and research purposes. They are studied by botanists and horticulturists to better understand the plant's biology, ecology, and evolution.

MEDICINAL USE

While Lithops are not known for their medicinal properties, they are sometimes used in traditional medicine practices. The plant has been used in some cultures to treat conditions such as arthritis, wounds, and digestive problems.

CULTURAL SIGNIFICANCE

Lithops are also significant in some cultures as a symbol of longevity, survival, and resilience. They are sometimes given as gifts to represent these qualities.

CREATING AN ATTRACTIVE LITHOPS DISPLAY

CHOOSING A CONTAINER

When creating an attractive display for your Lithops, it is important to choose a container that is both functional and aesthetically pleasing. Terracotta pots, shallow trays, and glass containers are popular choices for displaying Lithops. Choose a container that is slightly larger than your Lithops to allow for growth.

ARRANGING YOUR LITHOPS

Once you have chosen your container, arrange your Lithops in a way that is visually appealing. Consider color, shape, and texture when grouping your plants together. You can also add other decorative elements to your display, such as rocks or sand, to add visual interest.

POSITIONING YOUR LITHOPS

Lithops prefer bright, indirect light, so position your display in a location that receives plenty of natural light. However, be careful not to expose your Lithops to direct sunlight, as this can damage the plant. You should also avoid placing your display near cold drafts or heating vents.

CARING FOR YOUR LITHOPS DISPLAY

To keep your Lithops display looking its best, it is important to provide proper care. Water your Lithops sparingly, only when the soil has completely dried out. Use a well-draining soil mix and avoid getting water on the leaves, as this can cause the plant to rot. Additionally, fertilize your Lithops sparingly during the growing season. By following these tips, you can create a beautiful and attractive display for your Lithops that showcases the unique beauty of these fascinating plants.

IDEAL CONTAINERS FOR LITHOPS

SHALLOW AND WIDE CONTAINERS

Lithops have a shallow root system and require a container that is wide enough to accommodate their size but shallow enough to prevent water from accumulating around their roots. A container with a depth of 2-3 inches is ideal for Lithops.

DRAINAGE HOLE

Lithops are susceptible to root rot, and it is crucial to have a container with adequate drainage. A container with a drainage hole at the bottom is essential to prevent water from accumulating and causing root rot.

TERRACOTTA POTS

Terracotta pots are a good option for Lithops as they are porous and allow for proper air circulation and drainage. They are also affordable and readily available in most garden centers.

DECORATIVE CONTAINERS

While terracotta pots are the ideal choice for Lithops, decorative containers such as ceramic or glass pots can also be used as long as they have a drainage hole. It is essential to ensure that the container is not too deep, and the Lithops are not planted too deeply to prevent overwatering and root rot.

GROUPING LITHOPS

Lithops look great when planted in groups, and shallow containers can accommodate several Lithops. When grouping Lithops, it is essential to leave enough space between each plant to prevent overcrowding and allow for air circulation. Overall, the ideal container for Lithops is shallow and has adequate drainage. Terracotta pots are an excellent option, but decorative containers can also be used as long as they have a drainage hole and are not too deep. Grouping Lithops in shallow containers can create an attractive display.

LANDSCAPING WITH LITHOPS

INTRODUCTION

Lithops can be used to create beautiful and unique landscapes. These plants are drought-tolerant and can thrive in harsh environments. They are also relatively low maintenance, making them ideal for those who want a stunning landscape without a lot of upkeep.

DESIGN IDEAS

Lithops can be used in a variety of ways to create a beautiful landscape. Here are some design ideas:

ROCK GARDENS

Lithops look great in rock gardens. They can be planted amongst a variety of rocks and other succulents to create a stunning display.

CONTAINERS

Lithops are great for containers, especially when paired with other succulents. You can create a beautiful display by planting different varieties of lithops in a single container.

PATHWAY BORDERS

Lithops can also be used to create a border for a pathway. This is a great way to add interest to a pathway and create a stunning landscape feature.

LANDSCAPING TIPS

Here are some tips for landscaping with lithops:

PLANTING

When planting lithops, make sure to give them enough space to grow. They need at least a few inches of space between each plant.

WATERING

Lithops are drought-tolerant and do not need to be watered often. In fact, over-watering can be harmful to these plants. Make sure to let the soil dry out completely before watering again.

SOIL

Lithops need well-draining soil to thrive. Make sure to use a soil mix that is specifically designed for succulents.

LIGHTING

Lithops need plenty of sunlight to grow. Make sure to plant them in an area where they will receive full sun for most of the day.

CONCLUSION

Lithops are a great addition to any landscape. With their unique appearance and low maintenance needs, they are a great choice for those who want a stunning landscape without a lot of upkeep. Use these tips to create a beautiful lithops display in your own yard.

TIPS FOR SUCCESSFUL LITHOPS CULTIVATION

1. CHOOSE THE RIGHT SOIL MIX

Use a well-draining soil mix that consists of a combination of sand, perlite, and grit. This will ensure that the soil does not hold excess moisture and will prevent root rot.

2. PROVIDE THE RIGHT AMOUNT OF LIGHT

Lithops thrive in bright light, but direct sunlight can damage their leaves. Place them in a bright, sunny location with partial shade, especially during the hottest part of the day.

3. WATER SPARINGLY

Lithops are adapted to arid environments and require very little water. Only water them when the soil is completely dry, and be careful not to get water on their leaves, which can cause them to rot.

4. MAINTAIN THE RIGHT TEMPERATURE AND HUMIDITY

Lithops prefer warm temperatures and low humidity. Keep them in a warm location with good air circulation and avoid placing them in areas with high humidity, such as bathrooms.

5. FERTILIZE SPARINGLY

Lithops do not require much fertilizer. Use a low-nitrogen fertilizer once a month during their growing season (spring and summer), and avoid fertilizing them during the winter months when they are dormant.

6. AVOID OVERHANDLING

Lithops are delicate plants and can easily be damaged by overhandling. Handle them as little as possible and avoid touching their leaves, which can cause them to split or crack.

7. KEEP AN EYE OUT FOR PESTS AND DISEASES

Lithops can be susceptible to pests such as spider mites and mealybugs, as well as fungal diseases such as root rot. Inspect your plants regularly and take action if you notice any signs of infestation or disease.

CONCLUSION

In conclusion, Lithops are fascinating and unique succulents that are highly valued by collectors and gardeners alike. With their interesting shapes, colors, and patterns, they make great additions to any indoor or outdoor garden. However, successful cultivation of Lithops requires proper understanding of their specific needs and care requirements.

From understanding the origin and natural habitat of Lithops, to choosing the right soil mix, providing adequate watering and lighting, controlling temperature and humidity, and preventing pests and diseases, there are many factors to consider in order to ensure healthy and thriving plants.

Whether you are looking to propagate Lithops from seed or by grafting, it is important to have the right tools and knowledge to do so. Additionally, understanding the nutritional needs of Lithops and fertilizing them appropriately can help promote optimal growth and development.

With proper care and attention, Lithops can be enjoyed for many years to come, and can even provide culinary and medicinal benefits. Creating an attractive Lithops display, whether in containers or in landscaping, can also be a fun and rewarding project for plant enthusiasts.

Printed in Great Britain
by Amazon

24442429R00036